I AM PART OF NATURE

Written by Jenna Bayne
Illustrated by Riley Shortt

YOU ARE AMAZING!

Your body is so magnificent just the way it is. It performs such complex functions without you having to control any part of it. Regardless of the challenges you are facing right now, you have the infinite power of nature flowing through you which makes you more resilient than you could ever imagine. The physical aspects of your body, such as the color of your skin, the texture of your hair, the cellulite on your thighs or the laugh lines by your eyes are all beautiful parts of being alive and having a body. Embrace them! Respect and cherish the brilliance of your body by feeding it what it needs to thrive in order to live up to your full potential. You are such a significant and powerful force of nature. I am thrilled our paths have crossed on this life journey.

This is just 1 book in the BAYNE BOOK series. Find out more and connect with me at jennabayne.com where you will find all my social media handles, updates and personal notes from me to you. I can't wait to get to know you! A portion of total net earnings from each book are donated to 1Life Fully Lived and Front Row Factor Charites. Thank you for supporting the creation of an epic life!

DEDICATION

This book is dedicated to YOU. You've picked up this book, in this moment, because there is something in my words that you need to hear today. Read this book alone or cuddling up with someone you love while you are reminded to focus on the beauty of your nature. You are exquisite!

ACKNOWLEDGMENTS
(NOTE TO ADULTS)

First, I would like to acknowledge all the farmers out there in this world who supply our world with humanely-raised and organic foods. Your efforts and genuine souls are so appreciated. Thank you for all that you do!

Second, I want to acknowledge anyone who has ever struggled with food, weight or body-love. The dieting industry and food companies have really made healthy eating complicated. There are so many quick fixes, calorie rules, conflicting studies and complex opinions around what to eat, how much to eat and when to eat. What I have come to know and what traditional diets and experts fail to tell you is that none of this matters. No one knows your body better than you, so instead of looking outside yourself for the answers I encourage you to look within. Instead of beating yourself up for not having a "perfect" body, focus on the magnificence of your body. Focus on fulfilling nutrient deficiencies rather than calorie deficiencies. Restriction, deprivation and starvation will never make you happy or healthy. It is time we go back to the basics and put our trust back in our nature. This book supports every type of diet from vegan all the way to paleo and is by no means intending to favor one way of eating over another. The simple message is no matter what or how you choose to eat, ensure that it is as close to nature as possible and you will be setting yourself up for the best chance at great health.

Third, I'd like to honor all influencers of children. Your role is so important and not an easy task! It is challenging at times to get children to eat nature foods, so one of the intentions of this book is to support you with this endeavor. Read this affirmation book with children to bond and stimulate an open conversation around eating for vitality and health as well as body love. Low self-esteem often begins at a young age, so use this book as a resource to help your children discover and maintain an appreciation for the magnificence of their body. I encourage you to read this book with your children for a minimum of 21 days to ingrain a positive relationship to food, body and weight. Together we can dramatically reduce, if not eliminate, body dis-ease such as obesity and diabetes, as well as poor self-image in our future generations. It starts here. We are in this together!

Lastly, it is my greatest intention to spread body-love with this book. I want to acknowledge and remind my readers once more to really think about how fascinating the body really is. It is our shell that hosts our soul and without it we wouldn't be able to participate in this human experience. Your body is perfect no matter what size or shape. Think beyond the messages from external sources and go into your heart. Think of all things your body does for you. You can write with a pen on paper without consciously thinking about it. You can move any part of you in an instant. You blink, breathe and sneeze automatically to keep your system functioning optimally. Your body is so magical! And most of all, no matter how bad you treat it or talk about it, it still shows up for you. How do you treat your body in return for all it does for you? Show it love by remembering you are part of nature, and nature is beautiful. Hug yourself, kiss your biceps and smile every chance you have because you have a body, and that is worth celebrating!

I AM PART OF NATURE

Written by Jenna Bayne

Illustrated by Riley Shortt

I am part of nature
and nature is part of me!
I eat mostly nature foods
to be as healthy as I can be!

What I eat is important
because food is my fuel.
Eating foods that come from nature
is my number one rule!

I can eat in abundance
every vegetable under the sun.
This is the very reason
I am so fast when I run!

Nature foods have so many nutrients
that my body requires to succeed.
I will harness an intelligent mind
by giving my body what it needs.

Fruits come from nature
nuts and seeds do too!
Animal protein, eggs and seafood
are also great choices to consume.

Which foods are found in nature?

The body is complex
so, I invite you to come along.
You will learn about your body's needs
and what will keep you strong.

First, look down at both your hands.
Do you know what grows your nails?
Or what heals your skin when you get cut?
Have you ever thought of these details?

You see your body is magnificent!
It is amazing what it can do.
It does all these functions daily
without you having to tell it to!

You may wish to be taller
or have different skin or hair.
But, YOUR body is so magical
without you having to be aware.

Your body supports you always
and never asks for anything in return.
So embrace every part of your body
for compassion is what it yearns.

Your heart beats continually for you.
You breathe without a thought.
Your body is so brilliant
and it is the only one you've got!

SAY IT LOUD AND PROUD...

I am part of nature
and nature is part of me!
I eat mostly nature foods
to be as healthy as I can be!

What I eat is important
because food is my fuel.
Eating foods that come from nature
is my number one rule!

There was a time when humans ate
only what was hunted or gathered food.
Things like vegetables, fruits, nuts and seeds,
land animals and seafood.

Back then there weren't any factories
creating "convenience" foods.
There was only what nature offered us
within a particular altitude.

It depended on our environment,
what it was back then we ate.
Then we started farming
to help keep food upon our plates.

Grocery stores and restaurants
didn't exist like they do today.
Our way of life is so different.
Can you identify more ways?

Often today we fuel our bodies
with ingredients we don't know.
And even though our bodies keep evolving
they still require nature foods like long ago.

SAY IT WITH GUSTO...

I am part of nature
and nature is part of me!
I eat mostly nature foods
to be as healthy as I can be!

What I eat is important
because food is my fuel.
Eating foods that come from nature
is my number one rule!

The passionate farmers who authentically
and humanely grow our food,
who dedicate their life's work
to providing healthy food for me and you.

These are true heroes
for they provide nature foods for us to buy.
These farmers work so hard
to keep healthy food in our supply!

Because when we eat foods found in nature,
our bodies know exactly what to do.
When our cells are fueled properly
you become the healthiest version of you!

Body health is compromised
when it is filled with non-nature food.
Eating nature foods most of the time
will make you feel renewed.

To grow strong and healthy
you know what you need to do.
Eat an abundance of nature foods
and show your body you love it too!

How else can you love your body better?
What are some things that you could do?
How can you show yourself today
how much you cherish you?

Try looking into a mirror
while exclaiming, "I love you!"
Then give yourself a big hug
feeling full of body gratitude.

The most precious parts of nature
are those that are unique and rare.
No two pieces of nature are the same,
so there is no need to compare.

YOU are part of nature
and nature is magnificent,
thus, YOU too are just as amazing,
unique and significant!

REPEAT THIS AFFIRMATION DAILY...

I am part of nature
and nature is part of me!
I eat mostly nature foods
to be as healthy as I can be!

What I eat is important
because food is my fuel.
Eating foods that come from nature
is my number one rule!

ABOUT THE AUTHOR

Jenna Bayne is the size of a mouse but has the heart of a lion. She uses poetry to share her heart-felt thoughts, valued experiences and deepest wisdom. Her intention for creating her books is to remind her readers just how amazing they are, simply because they are them and part of this universe. Her dream is to become the next Dr. Seuss for her rhymes, brilliance and authenticity. Her passion is taking complex ideas and presenting them simply in an entertaining format to reach as many audiences as possible. She began as a classroom teacher while building her own on-line nutritional practice to stimulate healthy relationships with body, health and food. She now does this full time and truly believes in the power of eating nature foods for health, happiness and vitality. To connect with Jenna and learn more about her projects subscribe to jennabayne.com.

JENNA IS A FIRM BELIEVER IN GIVING BACK, SO A PORTION OF TOTAL NET EARNINGS FROM ALL BAYNE BOOK SALES WILL GO TO 1LIFE FULLY LIVED AND FRONT ROW FACTOR CHARITIES.

Thank you for being part of the conscious shift to self-appreciation and inner peace.

ABOUT THE ILLUSTRATOR

Riley Shortt is a Southwestern Ontario based artist who works largely with oil paint, water colour, charcoal and graphite. She primarily focuses her energies on portraits. She holds a Bachelor of Arts with Honours in Studio Art from the University of Guelph in Canada and a Graduate Diploma in Secondary Education from the University of the Sunshine Coast in Australia. Her art has appeared in juried art shows in Guelph as well as at Sarnia's Artist Co-Op and in the city's annual ArtWalk. When she is not painting, Shortt is teaching at the primary and high school level. She is based out of Sarnia, Ontario where she lives with her tabby cat, Finnegan.

BAYNE BOOKS®: Irresistibly Brilliant Book Series

Made in the USA
Middletown, DE
11 June 2017